Books are to be returned on or before
the last date below.

0

Fruit and Vegetables

Jenny Ridgwell

First published in Great Britain by Heinemann Library
Halley Court, Jordan Hill, Oxford OX2 8EJ,
a division of Reed Educational and Professional Publishing Ltd.

Heinemann is a registered trademark of Reed Educational and
Professional Publishing Ltd.

OXFORD FLORENCE PRAGUE MADRID ATHENS
MELBOURNE AUCKLAND KUALA LUMPUR SINGAPORE TOKYO
IBADAN NAIROBI KAMPALA JOHANNESBURG GABORONE
PORTSMOUTH NH (USA) CHICAGO MEXICO CITY SAO PAULO

Designed by Celia Floyd
Illustrations by Barry Atkinson, pp. 8, 14, 15, 16, 20, 24, 26, 28;
Oxford Illustrators, pp. 4, 6, 17, 18
Printed in Hong Kong

02 01 00 99
10 9 8 7 6 5 4 3 2

ISBN 0 431 08873 X

British Library Cataloguing in Publication Data

Ridgwell, Jenny
   Fruit and vegetables. - (Food in focus)
   1.Fruit - Juvenile literature   2.Vegetables - Juvenile
literature
   I.Title
   664.8

Acknowledgements

The Publishers would like to thank the following for permission to reproduce
photographs:

Gareth Boden, pp. 9, 10, 12, 13, 19, 21, 23, 25, 27, 29; Trevor Clifford, p. 22;
Liz Eddison, p.5; SIS Marketing, p. 11; Trip, p. 6 (V. Kolpakor); Zefa, p. 7

Cover photograph: Trevor Clifford

Contents

Introduction 4

Where are fruit and vegetables grown? 6

What are vegetables and fruits? 8

Keeping fruit and vegetables 10

Processing fruit and vegetables 12

Unusual fruit and vegetables 14

How is fruit juice made? 16

Choosing and cooking 18

Fruit, vegetables and health 20

Experiments with fruit and vegetables 22

Vegetable and noodle stir-fry 24

Summer pudding 26

Dried fruit salad with orange juice 28

Glossary 30

Further reading 31

Index 32

Some words are shown in bold, **like this**. You can find out what they mean by looking in the Glossary.

Introduction

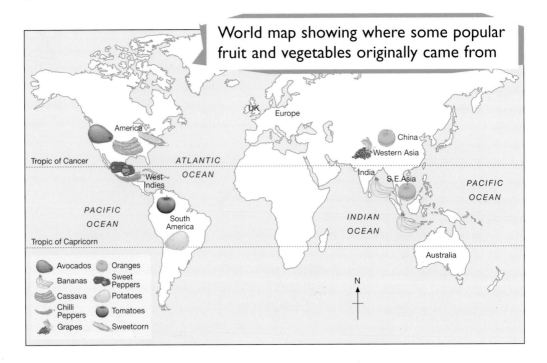

World map showing where some popular fruit and vegetables originally came from

Today there is a huge variety of fruit and vegetables for sale in our shops. They come in all shapes, sizes and colours, from all around the world. We need to eat plenty of fruit and vegetables as part of a healthy diet, as they are good sources of vitamins, minerals and fibre. **Starchy** root vegetables, such as potatoes and cassava, provide us with energy, and fresh fruit is a healthy snack food.

We have such a wide choice of fruit and vegetables today because explorers, settlers and traders have taken food plants on their travels. Plants that once only grew in one small region now thrive in many areas of the world. Potatoes and tomatoes are two of the world's most important food crops. These plants, as well as sweet peppers, chillies (all varieties of capsicums) and avocados originally came from South and Central America. Europeans first came to this continent, which they called the New World, about 600 years ago. They took plants back to Europe and other parts of the world. In return, settlers planted sugar cane, which came from the tropics of the Old World, and bananas which originally came from South East Asia in the New World.

Maize, or sweetcorn, was originally an American crop. It was brought to Europe by Columbus, the explorer, and is now widely grown around the world.

Plantains, which look like bananas, are used in cooking

The banana is one of the most popular fruits sold in our supermarkets. Bananas grow in parts of Australia, South Africa and the Caribbean, as well as tropical parts of Asia. This fruit can be eaten when it is sweet, or a starchy variety, known as plantain, is used in cooking.

The grape is one of the oldest cultivated fruits and probably came originally from western Asia. The Ancient Egyptians crushed grapes to make wine and dried them to make currants and raisins. The Greeks and Romans planted vineyards in their European colonies and wine is now made in many parts of the world.

Did you know?

To encourage children to eat more vegetables a UK food company is selling a range of Wacky Veg which includes chocolate-flavoured carrots, pizza-flavoured sweetcorn and baked-bean-flavoured peas!

Where are fruit and vegetables grown?

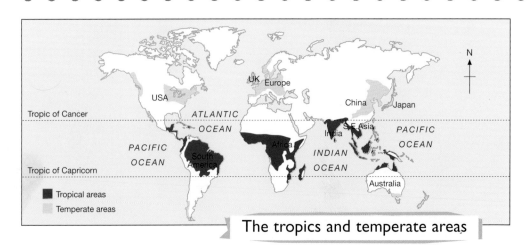

The tropics and temperate areas

Tropical areas
Temperate areas

Fruit and vegetables around the world

Different kinds of fruit and vegetables grow well in different climates.

Tropical food plants, such as pineapples, mangoes, papayas, avocados and bananas, grow in the hot, wet regions of the tropics which are found between the Tropic of Cancer and the Tropic of Capricorn.

Temperate areas, such as northern Europe, have a milder, cooler climate and grow **temperate food plants** such as apples, pears, cabbages and carrots. Apples are the most important fruit that grow in temperate regions and are a valuable winter food because they can be kept for a long time.

Oranges, lemons, tangerines, limes and grapefruit are all **citrus fruit**. They originally came from China, India and South East Asia. These fruits are grown in many parts of the world. The most important citrus fruit producing areas include Florida, California, the Mediterranean region, South Africa and Central America.

Apples grow well in temperate climates

Pineapples grow on plants which sprout from the ground

How do fruit and vegetables grow?

The main types of fruit and vegetables include peas, beans, apples, citrus fruit, bananas, leaf crops, such as cabbage and spinach, and root crops, such as potatoes, carrots, sweet potatoes and cassava.

Many fruits, such as plums, pears, apples and cherries, grow on trees. Soft summer fruits such as raspberries, gooseberries, blackcurrants and redcurrants grow on bushes.

Many salad vegetables and soft fruits are grown in large greenhouses. The glass protects the plants from damage from wind and rain, and allows in sunlight which is needed for the plants to grow.

Not all vegetables grow on land. Seaweed, which is a rich source of vitamins and minerals, is harvested from coastal sea waters. The Japanese are famous for eating seaweed and it can be used in salads and for wrapping foods like sushi.

Organic fruits and vegetables are grown without the use of chemicals for fertilizers and pest control. These fruits and vegetables are usually more expensive than those grown by other methods of farming, as it is more difficult to produce perfect, pest-free products.

People who eat **organic food** believe that it tastes better and is good for the environment.

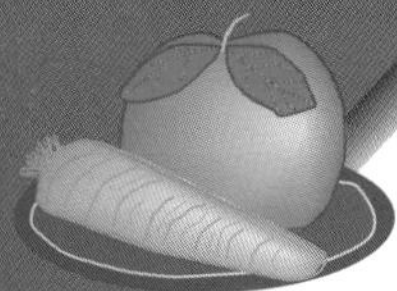

What are vegetables and fruits?

What is a vegetable?

Vegetables are plants that are used for food. Vegetables are usually eaten as part of the savoury course of a meal or snack. Different parts of the plants can be used as vegetables. The chart shows the parts of plants that we eat.

Parts of the plant	Examples
the whole plant above the ground 	beansprouts (bean shoots), asparagus, bamboo shoots
stems 	celery, rhubarb, fennel
leaves 	lettuce, spinach, cabbage, Chinese leaves (*po tsai* or Peking cabbage)
buds and flowers 	cauliflower, broccoli, Brussels sprouts
seeds 	peas, beans, lentils, *mange tout* (pea seeds in their pods, also called snow peas)
roots and tubers 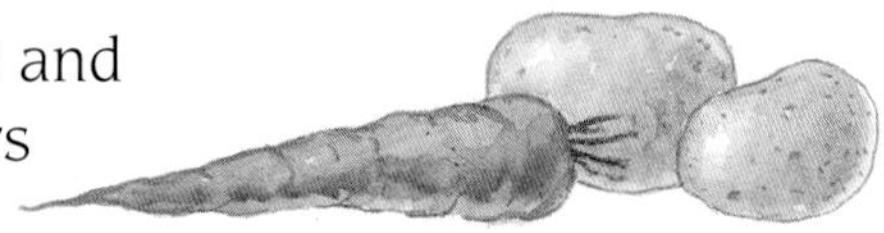	carrots, parsnips, potatoes, sweet potatoes
bulbs 	onions, leeks, garlic

Sometimes we eat all of the parts of the plant that grow above the ground, such as asparagus.

Leafy vegetables, such as cabbage, spinach and lettuce, also grow above the ground. They provide important nutrients including vitamin C, calcium, iron and fibre. Leafy vegetables can be served raw or cooked. Experts suggest that we should eat more vegetables raw, as nutrients such as vitamin C are lost in cooking.

Look carefully at cauliflower and broccoli and you will see that they are the flowers of the plant.

Plant **seeds**, such as beans, peas, sweetcorn and lentils, are good sources of protein, carbohydrate and fibre.

Roots and tubers are the parts of the plant that grow on or below the ground. Examples include carrots, parsnips, potatoes, cassava and sweet potatoes. These vegetables are good sources of **starch** and some fibre, especially in the outer skins.

Vegetable bulbs grow on or below the surface of the ground. They include onions, leeks and garlic. These vegetables are useful as they give flavour to other foods.

What is a fruit?

The scientific term for a fruit is 'the ripened **ovary** of the plant containing the seeds'.

Some fruits are used as vegetables. Marrows, pumpkins and cucumbers all contain seeds, so they are 'fruits'. Other fruits that we use as vegetables include green and red peppers (types of capsicum), tomatoes, avocado and aubergines (egg plants or *brinjal*).

Some fruits, such as plums, peaches and mangoes, contain one large stone. Other fruits, such as oranges and grapes, contain many seeds. Strawberries have their seeds on the outside skin.

Like vegetables, fruit is an important source of vitamin C and fibre. Orange and yellow fruit, such as apricots and bananas, contain vitamin A which is needed to keep our skin and body healthy.

Avocados and tomatoes are fruits which are served as vegetables

9

Keeping fruit and vegetables

For thousands of years people have found ways to **preserve** food to stop it going bad. Yeasts, moulds and bacteria cause food to change. To spoil food these micro-organisms themselves need food, warmth and liquid. **Enzymes** also cause food changes. Food is preserved by removing or preventing these micro-organisms from working.

Early ways to preserve fruit and vegetables include drying and pickling.

Drying

The Ancient Egyptians and Greeks dried grapes and used them for cooking and to make sweet snacks. Most grapes used in this way are dried into raisins by leaving them in the sun.

Many types of fruit and vegetable can be dried, including: beans, peas and lentils; fruits, such as apricots, pears, plums (which are dried to make prunes) and vegetables, such as mushrooms and potatoes. You can dry fruit and vegetables at home using an electric food dehydrator. Hot air rises through trays of food and removes 95% of the moisture content from the food. If the moisture is removed the micro-organisms cannot grow.

Dried fruits include prunes, figs, pears, apricots and raisins

Vegetables which can be pickled include cabbage, onions and gherkins

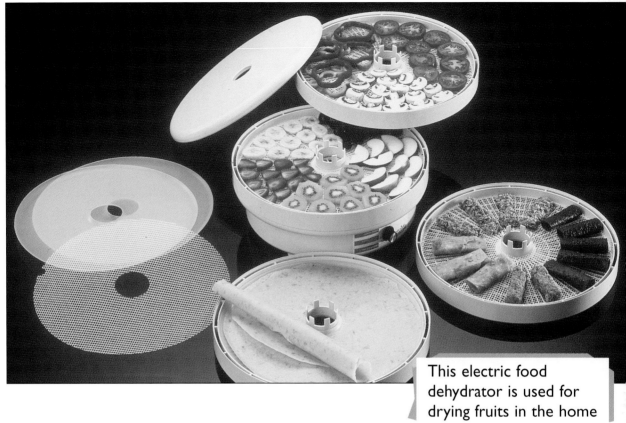

This electric food dehydrator is used for drying fruits in the home

Freeze-dried potatoes were invented by the Incas in South America. Potatoes froze at night in the cold air and dried in the hot sun by day. This dried potato could be stored for food for several years.

Accelerated freeze-drying is a modern system of drying food under **vacuum**, which means removing all the air, at reduced **pressure**. This method of drying causes little damage to the food. Today, many vegetables are freeze-dried in food factories, to help keep the colour and flavour. Some freeze-dried food products have been taken on space missions, as they will keep for a long time.

Pickling

Fruit and vegetables can be pickled by storing them in vinegar. In the Middle East, turnips, carrots and aubergines (egg plants) are pickled in spicy vinegar. Fruit is mixed with onions, spices and vinegar to make delicious chutneys which are served with cold meat and cheeses. The acid in the vinegar prevents the growth of micro-organisms.

One way to preserve soft summer fruits, such as strawberries and raspberries, is to make jam. Jam is a mixture of fruit, sugar and water which has been boiled and set. The acidity of the fruit and the high level of sugar prevent the growth of micro-organisms.

11

Processing fruit and vegetables

There are many modern ways of processing fruit and vegetables so that they will keep fresh for longer.

Canning

Fruit, such as peaches, apricots, mangoes and mandarins, can be **preserved** by canning. Food is placed in cans made of tinned steel, liquid added, and the can is sealed and heated until the micro-organisms are destroyed. Popular canned vegetables include peas, red kidney beans, sweetcorn and tomatoes.

Freezing

Most fruit and vegetables can be frozen in food factories. Food manufacturers claim that it takes only two hours to harvest, clean, prepare and freeze fruit and vegetables. Most food is quick-frozen as this fast freezing method results in smaller ice crystals forming. This causes less damage to the plant cells when the product is defrosted. Slow freezing breaks down the cell walls and changes the appearance of the food.

Irradiating

Foods can be **irradiated** by passing energy waves through the product to destroy micro-organisms. Not many foods are preserved by this method as it is expensive to carry out. Many people are concerned about the long-term effects of food preserved in this way.

Canning is a method of preserving vegetables

Modified atmosphere packaging

Prepared fruit and vegetables, such as salads and chopped fruit, have been washed and cut. They could change colour, lose moisture and become unpleasant to eat if they were not specially packed. **Modified atmosphere packaging** (**MAP**) or **gas packing** is a method of keeping food longer by changing the gas around the food, so that it is not like the normal composition of air. Modified atmosphere packaging changes the gases in the packaging, by increasing the amount of carbon dioxide gas. This helps to keep the fruit and vegetables fresh for longer.

If kept chilled, these products have a **shelf-life** of 5–35 days, compared to 2–7 days if they are packed in air.

We are eating more and more ready-prepared meals, many made from vegetables. Vegetables are processed to make canned and chilled soups. 'Veggie burgers' made from beans and vegetables are popular with vegetarians who do not eat meat-products such as beefburgers. Cook-chill meals, such as vegetable curry, are cooked, fast chilled and stored at low temperatures ready to be reheated for serving.

Modified atmosphere packaging changes the gas inside the packaging for fresh, leafy salads

Unusual fruit and vegetables

Fruit and vegetables are called by different names in the various countries where they are grown. Around the world, fruit and vegetables are used for both savoury and sweet dishes.

Papaya – also called pawpaw – is a yellowish fruit with sweet, pink flesh and black **seeds** in the centre. The unripe fruit can be shredded and eaten as a vegetable in salads, and the ripe fruit is served on its own or made into fruit salads.

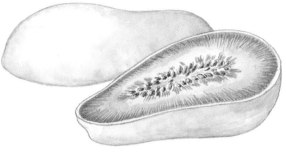

Christophene – also known as *chocho* (*choko*) – is a small, greenish, pear-shaped vegetable which is cooked and tastes like courgette (zucchini) or marrow. This vegetable is popular in Caribbean cooking.

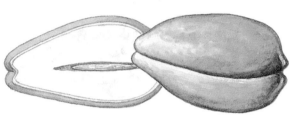

Sweet potato is a root vegetable with a pinkish skin and orange or white flesh. It can be boiled and roasted, and can also be made into sweet potato pie, which is a dessert.

Ackee is a fruit which is eaten as a vegetable. When ripe, the red fruits burst open and the yellowish flesh is eaten as a vegetable or made into salt fish and *ackee*.

The breadfruit gets its name because it tastes like bread. This large fruit has a thick, green rind and the flesh can be boiled, roasted or fried.

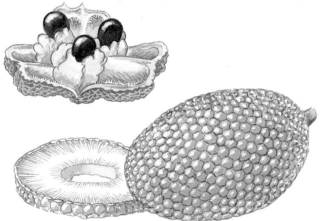

The lotus plant, which grows on lakes in China and Thailand, has many uses in cooking. The root is boiled or steamed and used in savoury dishes, and the leaves can be used to wrap food up for steaming.

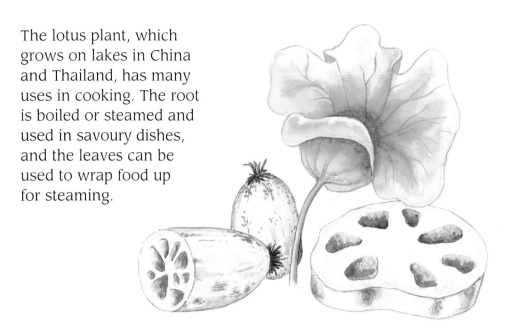

Water chestnuts are bulb-like vegetables which grow on shallow lakes and marshes. They are sliced and used to add crunchiness to salads and stir-fry dishes.

Genetic engineering

Scientists have found ways to change some plant foods. They alter the genes, which are the parts of every living thing that carry the plans for making new plants or animals that are similar to the parents. This process is called **genetic engineering**.

Flavr Savr R tomatoes were the first fresh food item on sale in the USA to have been genetically engineered. The tomatoes are picked when they are red and full of flavour. The softening gene has been 'switched off' so that tomatoes stay firm without going soft, and this makes transport and handling easier.

How is fruit juice made?

You can buy a wide range of fruit juices, but you need to look closely at the label to find out how they are made.

Three different methods of making fruit juice

Freshly squeezed juices are made from 100% fruit juice, containing no added water, colour, preservatives or sugar. The juices must be drunk within 2–3 days after purchase, otherwise the taste and texture change. These products must be chilled.

Fruit juices made from **concentrates** are 100% pure juice. Concentrate is fruit juice with most of the natural water removed by evaporation. The manufacturer adds water to this concentrate before packaging. These products can be chilled or, if they are **long-life products**, stored at **ambient temperature** (room temperature). They are less expensive than freshly squeezed juices, but some of the taste is lost during processing.

Concentrates are economical to transport around the world. The concentrate takes up less space as most of the water has been removed and this reduces transport and shipping costs and storage space. Concentrated fruit juice may be sold frozen. It can be made into a drink by defrosting it and adding water.

Fruit juice may also be sold in cans as well as plastic or glass bottles. The juice is sealed in a can, then heated to destroy micro-organisms which would cause the juice to deteriorate.

Fruit drinks are not made from 100% pure fruit juices. Water, flavourings, additives, sugar and preservatives can be added to these drinks, which may be chilled or long-life products.

How is a carton of fruit juice made?

Oranges are hand picked when ripe.

The oranges are sorted and cleaned in the factory.

The juice is squeezed from the oranges, then **pasteurized** to destroy micro-organisms which could cause the product to change.

The juice is chilled and sealed in special cartons which keep the juice fresh.

The product is ready for distribution around the world and is stored at 0–3°C. It has a chilled **shelf-life** of up to five weeks.

Choosing and cooking

Choose good quality, fresh vegetables and fruit and try to buy them locally when they are in season. Leafy vegetables should be green and not yellowing, and the leaves should not be damaged. Root vegetables should be firm and not limp, and not damaged by spade marks or the machinery used to remove the vegetables from the soil. Fresh vegetables are more nutritious than older vegetables and they taste better. Most salad vegetables, such as lettuce, celery and tomatoes, are best stored in the refrigerator. Root vegetables should be kept in a cool, dark place. Many vegetables can be eaten raw. Wash well before use. Some root vegetables, such as carrots, need peeling or scrubbing before being used.

There are many ways to cook vegetables to give flavour and colour, including barbecuing, steaming, stir-frying and cooking in the microwave oven.

Buy fresh and undamaged fruit which is firm and with no signs of mould. Most fruit is delicious eaten raw and just needs washing before eating.

Save the nutrients in fruit and vegetables

The nutrients in fruit and vegetables can be lost if they are not stored and cooked properly. Old or damaged fruit and vegetables lose vitamin C, so buy good quality, fresh produce and use it quickly.

Fibre and other nutrients are found in the skin, so avoid peeling fruit and vegetables. If possible, scrub root vegetables, such as carrots and potatoes, instead of peeling them.

Vitamin C is lost when fruit and vegetables are chopped up and when they are cooked for a long time, so prepare them when they are needed and don't leave them to stand about.

If vegetables are left to stand, or are cooked in water, the water-soluble vitamin C and the B-group vitamins will seep out into the water. Cook fruit and vegetables quickly in a little water and use the cooking water for sauces and gravies.

Fresh or processed – which is best?

Did you know that frozen or canned vegetables can be just as nutritious as fresh vegetables? Scientists have found that the amount of beta carotene (vitamin A), vitamin C and the B-vitamin niacin is the same in cooked vegetables, regardless of whether they were canned, frozen or fresh. This is because frozen or canned vegetables are processed within hours of harvesting, which helps to save their nutrients.

Fresh peas can be preserved by freezing and canning

Fruit, vegetables and health

Fruit and vegetables are important foods for a healthy diet. The **'healthy diet pyramid'** shows how to make healthy food choices. Our diet should contain a wide variety of different foods in order to provide the range of nutrients that we need.

The 'healthy diet pyramid' suggests that we eat plenty of **starchy** foods rich in dietary fibre, and lots of fruit and vegetables. These foods are shown in the lower section of the pyramid.

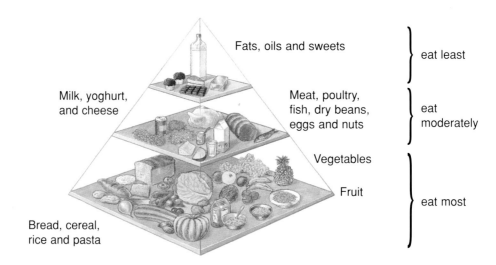

Experts suggest that for good health we should eat at least five servings of fruit and vegetables a day. This health message is known in many countries as 'Five a day'.

What do we mean by a serving?

The list shows serving sizes of fruit and vegetables according to the American National Cancer Institute. The American measure is shown in cups.

- 175 ml ($\frac{3}{4}$ cup) 100% fruit or vegetable juice
- 1 medium fruit, for example, apple, orange, banana, pear
- 40 g ($\frac{1}{4}$ cup) dried fruit
- 60 g (1 cup) raw leafy vegetables
- 160 g ($\frac{1}{2}$ cup) dry, cooked or canned peas or beans

Fruit and vegetables are very important for a healthy diet as they are good sources of vitamins, minerals and fibre. Generally fruit and vegetables contain little fat.

These are examples of the size of fruit and vegetable servings

Nutrients

Vitamins

Vitamins are essential for good health. Fruit and vegetables are our main source of vitamin C. Green, orange, yellow and red vegetables, such as green and red peppers (types of capsicum), carrots and leafy vegetables, supply us with vitamin A in the form of beta-carotene. Some B-group vitamins are present in green leafy vegetables.

Calcium and iron

Calcium is a mineral that is needed for strong bones and teeth, and iron is needed for healthy blood. Fruit and vegetables provide a little calcium, and dark green vegetables, such as spinach and broccoli, provide iron.

Fibre

Fruit and vegetables are sources of the fibre that is necessary to keep the digestive system healthy and to prevent constipation.

Carbohydrates

Fruit and vegetables contain some **complex carbohydrate** in the form of starch. It is found in root vegetables, such as potatoes, sweet potatoes and parsnips, and fruit, such as bananas. Sugar is found in fruit, such as apples, pears and tomatoes.

Protein

Some vegetables, such as peas, beans and lentils, provide protein.

Energy

Fruit and vegetables are made up of a lot of water. They do not provide us with much energy in the form of **calories**.

Experiments with fruit and vegetables

Some fruit and vegetables turn brown when they are cut and exposed to the air. This makes the fruit and vegetables look less attractive to eat. The change in colour happens when the fruit reacts with the oxygen in the air. This process, called **oxidation**, is due to the reaction – with oxygen – of an **enzyme** called polyphenol oxidase. An enzyme is a substance which takes part in a chemical reaction without changing itself. The browning of the fruit can be stopped if the fruit or vegetables are covered with lemon juice which contains vitamin C. The lemon juice is called an **anti-oxidant solution** since it prevents the enzyme from reacting with the oxygen and so stops the colour change in the fruit and vegetables.

Can you stop fruit changing colour?

You will need:

- 3 plates
- knife
- chopping board
- a choice of fruit such as apple, banana, pear, avocado
- water
- lemon juice

What to do:

1 Label the plates A, B and C.
2 Cut the pieces of fruit into equal slices and place a slice of each fruit on each plate.
3 Plate A – leave the fruit uncovered.
  Plate B – cover the fruit with a little water.
  Plate C – cover the fruit with lemon juice.
4 Leave the fruit for several hours and note the changes in colour.

Why do you add lemon juice to fruit salad?

You can see from this experiment that lemon juice helps prevent the fruit from turning brown. This is why you use lemon or orange juice to make a fresh fruit salad.

Why does red cabbage change colour?

Red cabbage will change colour if it is cooked or prepared in certain ways. The pigment in red cabbage is called **anthocyanin** which is a compound that gives the colour to red and purple fruit and vegetables. The pigment dissolves in liquid, such as water, and changes colour when it is mixed with an acid, such as vinegar or lemon juice. This is why pickled red cabbage is dark red. The cabbage pigment acts as an indicator, like litmus paper. This means it changes colour when it is mixed with an acid, such as vinegar, or an alkali, such as sodium bicarbonate. Cabbage pigment goes blue when mixed with an alkali.

Vegetable pigments can be used as a dye to add colour to fabrics, such as cotton, and to colour food products.

Changing the colour of red cabbage

You will need:

- chopping board
- sharp knife
- a small piece of red cabbage
- 2 bowls
- cold water
- tablespoon
- 2 tablespoons vinegar
- measuring jug
- sieve

What to do:

1 On a chopping board, cut the piece of cabbage in half. Cut each half into fine shreds and place into bowls labelled A and B.
2 Pour in enough cold water to cover the cabbage in bowl A.
3 Mix two tablespoons of vinegar with 500 ml of water and pour over the cabbage in bowl B.
4 Leave to stand for 10 minutes.
5 Strain the juice through a sieve. Compare the colours of each cabbage juice.

> Red cabbage changes colour when placed in vinegar

Before   After

Vegetable and noodle stir-fry

• •

You can use all kinds of vegetables for this stir-fry, which is based on a recipe from China. The Chinese cook food by stir-frying it in a wok, which is a curved metal pan. The food cooks very quickly and is stirred constantly, throughout cooking. Make sure the vegetables are thinly sliced so that they cook quickly. Vegetable and noodle stir-fry can be eaten as a main meal or as a snack. Before you start ask an adult to help.

Vegetable and noodle stir-fry

Serves 2

You will need:

Ingredients

- dried or fresh egg noodles – allow about 80–100 g of dried noodles and 100 g of fresh noodles per person
- approximately 300–400 g mixed raw vegetables – you can use carrots, mushrooms, *mange tout* (snow peas), red and green peppers (types of capsicum), baby sweetcorn, beansprouts (bean shoots), Chinese leaves (*po tsai*, Peking cabbage)
- 1 tablespoon oil
- 2 tablespoons soy sauce

Equipment

- sieve
- chopping board
- knife
- wok or large, deep frying pan
- tablespoon
- wooden spoon
- plate
- chopsticks

What to do:

1 Prepare the noodles according to the packet instructions. Dried noodles are usually soaked in boiling water for a few minutes, then drained and are ready to cook. Fresh noodles may need some cooking in boiling water or can be sold ready-cooked.

2 Wash the vegetables and prepare them for cooking. Peel the carrots. Slice the vegetables into thin strips – the beansprouts (bean shoots) are ready to use.

3 Heat the oil in the wok or frying pan. Take care with this stage of cooking as hot oil is dangerous. Fry the vegetables in the oil for two minutes, stirring all the time.

4 Add the cooked noodles and stir briskly for a further minute. Mix in the soy sauce.

5 Serve hot and eat with chopsticks.

Vegetable and noodle stir-fry

Summer pudding

This recipe is based upon a traditional English summer pudding which is made in the summer time when the fruit is ripe. The fruit is encased in bread, which soaks up the juices and turns a wonderful dark pink colour when left to stand for a few hours. You can use any soft summer fruit, such as strawberries, raspberries, black and redcurrants, and blackberries for this pudding.

Traditional English summer pudding

Serves 4

You will need:

Ingredients

- 650 g soft summer fruit, such as strawberries, raspberries and blackberries
- 50–75 g sugar to sweeten
- 8–10 large slices white bread

Equipment

- scales
- sieve
- bowl or saucepan with lid
- tablespoon
- knife
- chopping board
- 20 cm square cake tin or square or oblong dish
- plate and weight

What to do:

1 Pick over the fruit and remove any stalks and damaged fruit. Place in sieve and wash gently in running water to avoid damaging the fruit.
2 Cook the fruit until soft. There are two ways to do this.
  a) Place the fruit in a microwavable bowl and cover with plastic film. Cook for a few minutes until the fruit is soft. Stir occasionally. The cooking time will depend upon the type of fruit and the power of the microwave oven. Leave to cool slightly.

b) Place the fruit in a small saucepan with 3 tablespoons of water. Cover with a tight-fitting lid and simmer gently until the fruit is soft. Leave to cool slightly.

Stir the sugar into the fruit – add enough to sweeten to taste.

3 Using a knife, remove the crusts from the slices of bread and cut the bread into thick strips about 3–4 cm wide.

4 Press the strips of bread into the base and sides of the tin or dish.

5 Spoon the fruit into the bread-lined tin. Cover the top with more strips of bread. Place a clean plate on top of the summer pudding and put something heavy on top of the plate, such as a bag of sugar. This helps to press down the pudding and makes it firm. Leave in a cool place for several hours.

6 Remove the plate. Using a knife, loosen the sides of the summer pudding. Place a large plate on the top of the tin and turn the pudding upside-down onto the plate. Serve with yoghurt, ice-cream or fresh cream.

Summer pudding served with fresh cream

Dried fruit salad with orange juice

This recipe is based upon a traditional recipe which comes from the Middle East and uses a range of dried fruit. As you soak the fruits in orange juice they plump up and become juicy. You can buy many different kinds of dried fruit including prunes (which are dried plums), sultanas (dried grapes), pears, apricots, peaches and apples. Choose the ones that you like for this recipe.

Fruit salad with orange juice

Serves 2–4

You will need:

Ingredients

- 500 g mixed dried fruit, such as prunes, sultanas, apples, apricots, peaches and pears
- 500 ml orange juice
- 1 orange

Equipment

- scales
- measuring jug
- bowl
- saucepan with lid
- knife
- chopping board
- tablespoon

What to do:

1 Read the information on the dried fruit packet to find out if you need to soak the fruit before it is ready to use.
2 Place the pieces of dried fruit in a bowl with the orange juice. If the fruit needs soaking before it is ready to use, leave for the time given on the packet. If not, go straight to step 3.
3 Cook the fruit gently in the orange juice. Pour the fruit and orange juice into a saucepan, cover with a lid and simmer gently for 30 minutes. Test to see if the fruit is tender. If not, cook a little longer. Leave the mixture to cool slightly.
4 Remove the peel from the orange and cut the fruit into segments.
5 Mix the orange pieces with the dried fruit. If some of the dried fruit is in large pieces, cut into smaller pieces which are easier to eat.
6 Spoon the dried fruit salad in a bowl and serve with natural yoghurt or ice-cream.

Dried fruit salad with orange juice and ice-cream

Glossary

accelerated freeze-drying
drying food under vacuum
which causes very little damage

ambient temperature   room
temperature – a term used for
food storage

anthocyanin   a compound that
gives the colour to red and
purple fruit and vegetables

anti-oxidant solution   a
solution that prevents
substances from reacting with
oxygen

calories   units used to measure
the energy value of food

citrus fruit   oranges, lemons,
tangerines, limes and grapefruit

complex carbohydrate   a
carbohydrate in the form of
starch

concentrates   fruit juices with
most of the water removed. To
use, add water

enzyme   a substance that takes
part in a chemical reaction
without changing itself

gas packing   see *modified
atmosphere packing (MAP)*

genetic engineering   changing
the genes in plants to change
the qualities of the plant, such
as making tomatoes which do
not soften too quickly

healthy diet pyramid   a
system designed in the USA to
show how to make healthy
food choices

irradiation   a method of
preservation which destroys
micro-organisms by passing
energy waves through the food

long-life products   food
products that have been heat-
treated so that they can be
stored at room temperature and
last a long time without
deteriorating

**modified atmosphere
packaging** (**MAP**)   a way to
keep food longer by changing
the atmosphere around the
food so that it is not like the
normal composition of air

organic food   food is produced
without the use of pesticides
and fertilizers

ovary   the female part of the
flower in a plant

oxidation   reaction with
oxygen

pasteurization   heat-treatment
of foods to destroy micro-
organisms

preservation   methods to
prevent food from turning bad,
which include canning, freezing
and drying

pressure   the force produced
by pushing on something

roots and tubers   parts of
plants that grow underground,
such as carrots and potatoes

seeds the part of a plant that can be sown in the ground to produce new plants, examples include beans, peas and sweetcorn

shelf-life the length of time a product stays fresh when stored

starch carbohydrate found in food, used for energy

temperate food plants food plants grown in areas with cool climates, such as northern Europe

tropical food plants food plants grown in the tropics, between the Tropics of Cancer and Capricorn

vacuum a space from which all the air has been removed

Further reading

Focus on Fruit. Graham Houghton. Wayland Publishers, 1986

Food Around the World. Jenny Ridgwell and Judy Ridgway, Oxford University Press, 1986

Healthy Eating, Recipes and Investigations, Jenny Ridgwell and Judy Ridgway, Oxford University Press, 1989

Skills in Home Economics: Food. Jenny Ridgwell. Heinemann Educational, 1990

Index

Accelerated freeze-drying   11

Bulbs   8

Calcium   21
Canning   12
Carbohydrates   21
Chutneys   11
Citrus fruit   6

Dried fruit salad with orange
   juice   28, 29
Drying   10, 11

Experiments   22, 23

Fibre   21
Five a day   20
Flavr Savr R tomatoes   15
Flowers   8
Freeze-dried foods   11
Freezing   12
Fruit and vegetables, choosing
   18, 19
Fruit and vegetables, cooking
   18, 19
Fruit and vegetables, fresh
   18,
Fruit and vegetables, unusual
   14, 15
Fruit juice   16, 17

Genetic engineering   15
Grapes   5

Healthy diet pyramid   20

Irradiation   12

Jam   11

Leafy vegetables   9

Modified atmosphere
   packaging (MAP)   13

Nutrients   18, 19, 21

Organic foods   7

Pickling   10, 11
Plants, parts   8
Plants, temperate food plants   6
Plants, tropical food plants   6
Preserving   10, 11, 12, 13
Protein   21

Quick freezing   12

Ready meals   13
Roots   8

Seaweed   7
Seeds   8
Summer pudding   26, 27

Tubers   8

Vegetable and noodle stir-fry
   24, 25
Vitamins   18, 19, 21